Paul Muldoon was born in Northern Ireland in 1951 and educated at Queen's University, Belfast. He worked for thirteen years as a BBC radio producer, before moving to the USA, where he now teaches at Princeton. His last collection of poems, *The Annals of Chile*, was awarded the T. S. Eliot Prize in 1995. His *New Selected Poems 1968–1994* appeared in 1996 and won the Irish Times Literature Prize.

by the same author

NEW WEATHER
MULES
WHY BROWNLEE LEFT
QUOOF
MEETING THE BRITISH
MADOC: A MYSTERY
SHINING BROW
THE ANNALS OF CHILE
NEW SELECTED POEMS 1968–1994

THE FABER BOOK OF CONTEMPORARY IRISH POETRY (editor)
THE FABER BOOK OF BEASTS (editor)

for children

THE LAST THESAURUS
THE NOCTUARY OF NARCISSUS BATT

PAUL MULDOON Hay

faber and faber

First published in 1998
by Faber and Faber Limited
3 Queen Square London WC1N 3AU

Photoset by Wilmaset Ltd, Wirral
Printed in England by Mackays of Chatham plc, Chatham, Kent

A CIP record for this book
is available from the British Library

ISBN 0-571-19551-2

10 9 8 7 6 5 4 3 2

Contents

Acknowledgements

Acknowledgements are due to the editors of the following: *The American Scholar*, *The Atlanta Review*, *Blue Metropolis*, *Brangle*, *College Green*, *Columbia*, *Fence*, *The Guardian*, *Harvard Magazine*, *The Harvard Review*, *The Honest Ulsterman*, *Icarus*, *The Irish Review*, *Janus*, *The Kenyon Review*, *The London Review of Books*, *Metre*, *The Michigan Quarterly Review*, *The New Republic*, *New Writing 7*, *The New York Times*, *Notre Dame Review*, *The Oxford Quarterly Review*, *P.N. Review*, *Pequod*, *Poetry Daily* (World Wide Web), *Poetry Ireland Review*, *Poetry Review*, *Press*, *Princeton University Library Chronicle*, *The Sunday Times*, *The Sycamore Review*, *The Sydney Morning Herald*, *Tabla*, *The Times Literary Supplement*, *U.S.1*, *Verse* and *Writing Ulster*; also to the Australian Broadcasting Corporation, the British Broadcasting Corporation, National Public Radio and Radio Telefis Eireann.

'Errata', 'Hay', 'Paunch', 'Symposium', 'The Train' and 'Wire' first appeared in *The New Yorker*. 'Apple Slump' and 'The Throwback' first appeared in *Poetry*.

'The Point' was privately printed by The Gallery Press to celebrate a visit to Japan in 1994, 'A Half-Door near Cluny' as a Christmas poem in 1997. 'Plovers' and 'The Fridge' first appeared in *Kerry Slides*, also published by The Gallery Press, with photographs by Bill Doyle. The version of 'Rainer Maria Rilke: *The Unicorn*' was written in celebration of Ted Hughes's sixty-fifth birthday and published by Faber and Faber in *A Parcel of Poems*. Some sections of 'Sleeve Notes' appeared in *My Generation: Rock 'n' Roll Remembered*, published by Lilliput Press. 'Hopewell Haiku' was published in a limited edition by Warwick Press. 'The Little Black Book' appears in *Ravishing Disunities: An Anthology of Real Ghazals*, the getaway car 'Rune' in *New Exeter Riddles*. 'Third Epistle to Timothy' was the 1997 Phi Beta Kappa poem at Harvard University. 'The Bangle (Slight Return)' was published in a limited edition by the Typography Studio, Princeton.

Hay

The Mud Room

We followed the narrow track, my love, we followed the narrow
    track through a valley in the Jura
to where the goats delight to tread upon the brink
of meaning. I carried my skating-rink,
the folding one, plus
a pair of skates laced with convolvulus,
you a copy of the feminist Haggadah
from last year's seder. I reached for the haggaday
or hasp over the half-door of the mud room
in which, by and by, I grasped the rim
not of a quern or a chariot wheel but a wheel
of Morbier propped like the last reel
of *The Ten Commandments* or *The Robe*.
When she turned to us from high along the scarp
and showed us her gargoyle-
face stained with red-blue soil,
I could have sworn the she-goat was walking on air,
bounding, vaulting, pausing in mid-career
to browse on a sprig of the myrtle of which she's a
    devotee,
never putting a foot
wrong as she led us through the atrium's
down jackets, bow and quiver, jars of gefilte fish and
    garum,
to the uplands
where, at dusk, a farmer spreads a layer of bland
curds on the blue-green seam
of pine ash that runs like a schism

between bland dawn-milk and bland dusk-milk, along a
    corridor
smoking with the blue-green ordure
of cows, to yet another half-door that would issue
on to the altar of Jehovah-nissi.
There our kittens, Pangur Ban and Pyewacket,
sprawled on the horse-hair blanket I bought in Bogotá
along with the horse-hair hackamore.
There a wheel-felloe of ash or sycamore
from the quadriga to which the steeds had no sooner
    been hitched
than it foundered in a blue-green ditch
with the rest of the Pharaoh's
war-machine was perfectly preserved between two
    amphoras,
one of wild birdseed, the other of Kikkoman.
It was somewhere in this vicinity that I'd hidden the
    afikoman
at last year's seder. I looked back down the Valley of the
    Kings
that was flooded now by the tears of things
and heard again that she-goat pipe
home a herd of cows, their hullabaloo and hubbub
at dawn or dusk, saw again her mouth stained with
    fraochans
(for she is of blaeberry-browsers the paragon)
and followed her yet again through gefilte fish and
    garum jars,
crocks, cruses, saucepans, the samovar
from turn-of-the-century
Russia, along the blue-green path of pine cinders
through the myrtleberry – myrtle- or whortleberry? –
    underbrush

from which an apprehensive thrush
gave over its pre-emin ... pre-emin ... pre-emin ...
its pre-eminent voice to *une petite chanson
    d'Allemagne.*
There, in the berry-laden scrub,
was a brangle of scrap
that had once been the body of that quadriga.
Yet again I stood amid the drek
and clutter
of the mud room, the cardboard boxes from K-Mart and
    Caldor,
the hoover, the ironing-board, the ram's horn
on which Moses called to Aaron, a pair of my da's boots
    so worn
it was hard to judge where the boots came to an end
and the world began, given how one would blend
imperceptibly into the other, given that there was no
    fine
blue-green line
between them. Virgil's *Georgics.* Plato's *Dialogues.*
Yet again the she-goat reared up on her hind legs
in the Jura or the Haute-Savoie
and perched on top of that amphora of soy
and stared across the ravine
that, imperceptibly, intervenes
between the stalwart curds of daybreak
onto which the farmer rakes
the pine-coals from the warm hearthstone
and the stalwart curds of dailygone.
She reared up on her hind legs as if to see, once and for
    all,
the Children of Israel negotiate the water-wall
on their right hand

and on their left – 'Look, no hands' –
as if a she-goat might indeed pause in mid-career to
    browse
on some horse-hair blanket I bought in Valparaíso,
on a whirligig, a scythe and strickle, a cobbler's last.
They weighed on me now, the skating-rink and the
    skates laced
with convolvulus as we followed the narrow track, my
    love,
to that rugged enclave
in the Jura, to where a she-goat might delight to tread
upon the middle cake of matzo bread
that runs as neat as neat
between unleavened morning and unleavened night.
Yet again that she-goat had run ahead
and yet again we followed her through the Haute-
Savoie past a ziggurat
of four eighty-pound bags of Sakrete,
on the top of which she paused to expose her red-blue
    tongue,
past the hearth-set of brush, tongs
and poker bent
out of shape, past a shale outcrop of some of the pre-
    eminent
voices of the seventies – *The Pretender*, *Desperado*,
The Best of Spirit,
box after cardboard box
of all manner of schmaltz and schlock from Abba to
    Ultravox,
till we heard the she-goat's own pre-eminent voice
from across the blue-green crevasse
that ran between the cohorts of dawn and the dusk-
    cohorts,

heard her girn and grate
upon the mishugas
of the brazen-mouthed cows
of morn and the brazen-mouthed cows of even,
their horns summoned up by a seven-
branched candlestick itself once or twice summoned up
  at Shabbat.
The candelabrum, the whirligig, those boots
with their toes worn through from the raking of pine-
  coals
at crack of dawn and crepuscule,
the whirr of the bellows
and the dull glow
of pine-ash, the hubcap from a Ford Sierra
blown up in – yes, sirree –
a controlled explosion in Belfast, the Kaliber six-pack,
the stack of twenty copies of *The Annals of Chile* ($21
  hardback).
Again the she-goat would blare down the trail
when we paused to draw breath, as the Children of Israel
might draw breath on the Sabbath,
again exhort us to follow the narrow path
that runs like a blue-green membrane
between the amphoras of soy and assorted small-headed
  grains,
exhort us yet again to follow
through the valley
'the narrow track to the highest good' as set forth by
  Epicurus,
past the hearth-set of brush, tongs and poker
bent out of shape, the ever-so-faint scent of musk,
till I happened upon the snow-swatch of damask
in which I'd wrapped the afikoman. The bag of pitons.

The medicinal bottle of poteen.
Yet again something had come between
the she-goat poised on a slope on which the cattle batten
and ourselves, that rivulet
or blue-green fault
between the clabber of morn and the stalwart even-
    clabber.
It was time, I felt sure, to unpack the Kaliber
into the old Hotpoint fridge
in which the she-goat was wont to forage,
to toss the poster tube – Hopper, Magritte, Grant Wood –
and clear a space in the dew-wet
underbrush in which, at long last, I might open
my folding skating-rink and, at long last, tread upon
the hubcap of that old Sierra that could itself turn
on a sixpence, could itself turn
as precipitously as a bucket of milk in a booley-byre,
to roll up the strand of barbed wire
hand-wrought by the King of the Chaldeans,
the one and only Joseph Glidden,
that had run between the herd
of morn and the herd
of even, when you found the little *shuinshu* covered
    with black brocade
I bought for two zuzim our last day in Kyoto
and it struck me that the she-goat
had somehow managed to acquire what looked like your
    skates
and your *gants en chevreau*
and was performing grand jetés on the hubcap of the
    Ford Zephyr.
I, meanwhile, was struggling for a foothold.
Even as I drove another piton to the hilt

in the roughcast
of a bag of Sakrete, the she-goat executed an exquisite
saut de l'ange from an outcrop of shale,
pausing to browse on a sprig of myrtle or sweetgale
in the vicinity of the bow and quiver, down jackets,
    hoover,
where I hid the afikoman last Passover,
bounding, vaulting, never making a slip
as I followed her, then as now – though then I had to
    schlep
through the brush of skirts (maxi- and mini-)
my folding rink plus my skates laced with scammony
plus the middle of the three
cakes of matzo bread that had, if you recall, since gone
    astray.
It was time, I felt sure, to unpack the Suntory
into the old fridge, to clear a space between *De Rerum
    Natura*
and Virgil's *Eclogues*,
a space in which, at long last, I might unlock
the rink, so I drove another piton into an eighty-pound
bag of Sakrete and flipped the half-door on the dairy-
    cabinet
of the old Hotpoint
and happened, my love, just happened
upon the cross-
section of Morbier and saw, once and for all, the
    precarious
blue-green, pine-ash path along which Isaac followed
    Abraham
to an altar lit by a seven-branched candelabrum,
the ram's horn, the little goat-whirligig
that left him all agog.

The Point

Not Sato's sword, not Sato's 'consecrated blade'
that for all its years in the oubliette
of Thoor Ballylee is unsullied, keen,
lapped yet in the lap of a geisha's gown.

Not the dagger that Hiroo Onoda
would use again and again to undo
the frou-frous, the fripperies, the Fallopian
tubes of a dead cow in the Philippines.

What everything in me wants to articulate
is this little bit of a scar that dates
from the time O'Clery, my school-room foe,

rammed his pencil into my exposed *thigh*
(not, as the chronicles have it, my calf)
with such force that the point was broken off.

Nightingales

I

'In great contrast to the nightingale's pre-eminent voice
is the inconspicuous coloration of its plumage,'
as Alfred Newton so winningly puts it

in his *Dictionary of Birds*. I fell in love with a host-face
that showed not the slightest blemish.
They tell me her make-up was powdered nightingale-
   shit.

II

They tell me the Japanese nightingale's not a
   nightingale
but a Persian bulbul. Needless to say, it's the male bird
that's noted for opening the floodgates
and pouring out its soul, particularly during nesting
   season.

III

Now they tell me a network of wedges and widgets and
   wooden nails
has Nijojo Castle's floorboards
twitter 'like nightingales'. This twittering warned the
   shogunate
of unwelcome guests. Wide boys. Would-be assassins.

Plovers

The plovers come down hard, then clear again,
for they are the embodiment of rain.

The Bangle

I

Between the bream with cumin and the beef with
   marrow
in 'Le Petit Zinc'
a bangle gleamed. Aurora Australis.
Many a bream, my darling, and many a luce
in stew.

II

      Not unlike the magpie and the daw,
the emu loves a shiny doodah,
a shiny doodlebob.

III

      So a harum-scarum
bushman, hey, would slash one forearm
with a flint, ho, or a sliver of steel
till it flashed, hey ho, like a hel-
iograph.

IV

      By dribs, hey, by dribs and drabs
the emu's still lured from its diet of fruit and herbs
with a bottle-cap, ho, or a bit of tinfoil
till it's in the enemy's toils.

V

Its song ranges from a boom to a kerplink
reminiscent of the worst excesses of Conlon Nancarrow.

The Plot

He said, my pretty fair maid, if it is as you say,
I'll do my best endeavours in cutting of your hay,
For in your lovely countenance I never saw a frown,
So my lovely lass, I'll cut your grass, that's ne'er been
* trampled down.*

Traditional ballad

```
a l f a l f a l f a l f a l f a l f a
l f a l f a l f a l f a l f a l f a l
f a l f a l f a l f a l f a l f a l f
a l f a                     a l f a
l f a l                     l f a l
f a l f                     f a l f
a l f a         a l p h a   a l f a
l f a l                     l f a l
f a l f                     f a l f
a l f a                     a l f a
l f a l f a l f a l f a l f a l f a l
f a l f a l f a l f a l f a l f a l f
a l f a l f a l f a l f a l f a l f a
```

Tract

I cleared the trees about my cabin, all
that came within range of a musket ball.

Rainer Maria Rilke: *The Unicorn*

This, then, is the beast that has never actually been:
not having seen one, they prized in any case
its perfect poise, its throat, the straightforward gaze
it gave them back – so straightforward, so serene.

Since it had never been, it was all the more
unsullied. And they allowed it such latitude
that, in a clearing in the wood,
it raised its head as if its essence shrugged off mere

existence. They brought it on, not with oats or corn,
but with the chance, however slight,
that it might come into its own. This gave it such
  strength

that from its brow there sprang a horn. A single horn.
Only when it met a maiden's white with white
would it be bodied out in her, in her mirror's full length.

White Shoulders

My heart is heavy. For I saw Fionnuala,
'The Gem of the Roe', 'The Flower of Sweet Strabane',
when a girl reached down into a freezer bin
to bring up my double-scoop of vanilla.

Green Gown

In the afternoon my wife and I had a little quarrel which
I reconciled with a flourish. Then she read a sermon in
Dr Tillotson to me. It is to be observed that the flourish
was performed on the billiard table.
                    William Byrd, diary entry for July 30th, 1710

Again and again, when it came her turn
to take a shot,
Marie's first inclination had been to pass
for she knew full well that as soon as she bent low
over the table I would draw
closer to glimpse her 'two young roes

that were twins' and the 'ivory
tower' of her neck and shoulder and side
and the small of her back
and maybe even the flat
of her belly ... 'The poets of *Sir Gawayne
and the Grene*

Knight and *The Romance of the Rose*
were among those to whom Spenser would turn
and upon whom he would draw...'
It was the week after the Aldershot
bomb and we were all lying low
for fear of reprisals from Donegall Pass

and Sandy Row ... 'The description of a "greene
gowne" sported by Lecherie in *The Faerie
Queene*,
for example...' That vodka on the side
gave my glass of Heineken, which had fallen flat,
a little bit of pep ... Knock it back...

Knock it back, Rainer, till you pass
out on a breast dripping Liebfraumilch or Mateus Rosé
or Hirondelle ... 'If John Livingston Lowes
is to be believed, Coleridge's turn
of mind was that of a man who's half-shot
most of the time...' The main draw-

back,
then, of her house on College Green
had been that it was indeed a house, not a flat,
so that a gay Lothario
had to contend with the snide asides
of her Derry duennas ... Again and again

Dolores and Perpetua would gallop down a draw
and cut me off at the pass...
Again and again I'd been shot
down in flames ... Until this evening, when I rose
to find my Princess Marie von Thurn
und Taxis-Hohenlohe

sitting on the stately pile of old issues of *Gown*
they used, I'm quite sure, for wiping their back-
sides,
tipping a bottle of green
stuff on to her left palm ... 'Be it Fauré's
Andante for Violin and Piano in B flat

or his *Au bord de l'eau*,
his music fills me with longing...' You must draw
your own conclusions as to why things took this turn
after a month-long impasse,
but I suspect that I rose
in her estimation that afternoon when shot

after shot had rung out from Divis Flats
and I kept right on drinking my glass of Heineken
in the public bar of Lavery's
as if this was nothing more than a car back-
firing ... In any event, I was slumped, green
at the gills, over the side

of the toilet bowl, when she shot
me a glance such as Daphne might shoot Apollo:
'We must gather the Rose
of love, whilst yet is time.' 'Time?' 'To withdraw...'
It had already given her a little pizzazz,
that vodka, emboldened her to turn

the cue, hard, as she struck the ball, lending it such side
that it hurtled across the bogs, fens, flats
of chalky green
all the way from Aquinas to (if I may) Quine
at whom it baulked, wheehee, did some class of a back-
flip, then rebounded off Porphyry

and Averroes ... 'I use "withdraw"
in the Marvellian sense...' Spermicide, was it, or aloe
   vera?
'You'll be lucky to get an "allowed pass"...'
She lay on the flat of her back
in a haze of shot silk ... 'Since you've not done a hand's
   turn...'
Her breast ... 'Not a stroke...' The green of her green
   gown.

Now, Now

I

A sentence of death, my love, as if we were destined to
   squint
into the glint
of a firing party, going down on one knee
the better to see
their hearts a-flutter with swatches of lint.

II

Seeing, instead, a pig's back all tinges and tints
merely by dint
of its having been handed down, under an apple-heavy
   tree,
a sentence of death.

III

For we hold in our heart of hearts, as the frizzens strike
   their flints,
what we hitherto took as a hint –
that the rider whom we so eagerly
awaited will leap from the saddle now, now to issue the
   decree
that life is indeed no more than 'a misprint
in the sentence of death'.

Longbones

When she came to me that night in Damascus Street
she was quite beside herself. Her father was about to die
and his mirror was covered with a sheet

so his spirit might not beat
against it but fly as spirits fly.
When she came to me that night in Damascus Street

Longbones had driven through freezing rain or sleet
all the way from Lurgan. The Lurgan sky
was a mirror covered with a sheet

or a banner trailed by an army in defeat.
Though Longbones was already high
when she came to me that night in Damascus Street

she immediately shook out a neat
little blue or red cartouche until, by and by,
she had covered a mirror with a sheet

of that most valiant dust. Then she would entreat
me not to leave her, as if I
had come to her that night in Damascus Street,

as if I had asked if I might turn up the heat
and tested if the spare bed was dry
by slipping the mirror between the sheets.

Only when she turned to greet
me, wistful and wry,
that night of nights in Damascus Street,

did I remark on the discreet
blue or red teardrop tattooed under her left eye.
She covered the mirror with a sheet

and whispered, 'Come, my sweet,'
in a tone as sly as it was shy,
'come to me now.' That night in Damascus Street

was the last time Longbones and I would meet.
Only later did it strike me why
she would cover the mirror with a sheet.

Only when I looked back on her snow-white feet
and her snow-white thigh
did it come to me, next morning in Damascus Street,
that she herself was the mirror covered with a sheet.

Lag

We were joined at the hip. We were joined at the hip
like some latter-day Chang and Eng,
though I lay in that dreadful kip
in North Carolina while you preferred to hang

loose in London, in that self-same
'room in Bayswater'. You wrapped yourself in a flag
(the red flag, with a white elephant, of Siam)
and contemplated the time lag.

It was Chang, I seem to recall, who tried to choke
Eng when he'd had one over the eight.
It was Chang whose breath was always so sickly-sour.

It was Chang who suffered a stroke.
Eng was forced to shoulder his weight.
It was Chang who died first. Eng lived on for five hours.

Symposium

You can lead a horse to water but you can't make it
    hold
its nose to the grindstone and hunt with the hounds.
Every dog has a stitch in time. Two heads? You've been
    sold
one good turn. One good turn deserves a bird in the
    hand.

A bird in the hand is better than no bread.
To have your cake is to pay Paul.
Make hay while you can still hit the nail on the head.
For want of a nail the sky might fall.

People in glass houses can't see the wood
for the new broom. Rome wasn't built between two
    stools.
Empty vessels wait for no man.

A hair of the dog is a friend indeed.
There's no fool like the fool
who's shot his bolt. There's no smoke after the horse is
    gone.

Between Takes

I was standing in for myself, my own stunt double,
in a scene where I was meant to do a double

or maybe even a triple back-somersault
off the bed. In one hand she held a glass of Meursault,

in the other something akin to a Consulate.
When she spoke, she spoke through the consolette

in a diner booth where Meatloaf and The Platters
still larded it over those meatloaf platters

with all the trimmings. This was a moment,
it seemed, of such moment

that she felt obliged to set down both cigarette and glass
and peer as through the limo's tainted glass

for a glimpse of the mountain stream that, bolder and
   bolder,
did its little bit of laundry among the boulders.

Sleeve Notes

MICK JAGGER: Rock music was a completely new musical form. It hadn't been around for ten years when we started doing it. Now it's forty years old.

JANN S. WENNER: What about your own staying power?

MICK JAGGER: I have a lot of energy, so I don't see it as an immediate problem.

JANN S. WENNER: How's your hearing?

MICK JAGGER: My hearing's all right. Sometimes I use earplugs because it gets too loud on my left ear.

JANN S. WENNER: Why your left ear?

MICK JAGGER: Because Keith's standing on my left.

'Jagger Remembers', *Rolling Stone*, March 1996

THE JIMI HENDRIX EXPERIENCE:
Are You Experienced?

'Like being driven over by a truck'
was how Pete Townshend described the effect
of the wah-wah on 'I Don't Live Today'.

This predated by some months the pedal
Clapton used on 'Tales of Brave Ulysses'
and I'm taken aback (jolt upon jolt)
to think that Hendrix did it all 'by hand'.

To think, moreover, that he used *four*-track
one-inch tape has (jolt upon jolt) evoked
the long, long view from the Senior Study
through the smoke, yes sir, the smoke of battle
on the fields of Laois, yes sir, and Laos.

Then there was the wah-wah on 'Voodoo Child
(Slight Return)' from *Electric Ladyland*.

CREAM: *Disraeli Gears*

As I labored over the 'Georgiks and Bukolikis'
I soon learned to tell thunder from dynamite.

THE BEATLES: *The Beatles*

Though that was the winter when late each night
I'd put away Cicero or Caesar
and pour new milk into an old saucer
for the hedgehog which, when it showed up right

on cue, would set its nose down like that flight
back from the US ... back from the, yes sir...
back from the ... back from the USSR...
I'd never noticed the play on '*album*' and 'white'.

THE ROLLING STONES: *Beggar's Banquet*

Thanks to Miss Latimore,
I was 'coming along nicely' at piano

while, compared to the whoops and wild halloos
of the local urchins,

my diction
was im-pecc-a-ble.

In next to no time I would be lost
to the milk-bars

and luncheonettes
of smoky Belfast,

where a troubadour
such as the frontman of Them

had long since traded in the lute
for bass and blues harmonica.

VAN MORRISON: *Astral Weeks*

Not only had I lived on Fitzroy Avenue,
I'd lived there with Madame Georgie Hyde Lees,
to whom I would rather shortly be wed.

Georgie would lose out to The George and El Vino's
when I 'ran away to the BBC'
as poets did, so Dylan Thomas said.

It's the house in all its whited sepulchritude
(not the palm tree against which dogs piddle
as they make their way back from wherever
it was they were all night) that's really at a list.

Through the open shutters his music, scatty, skewed,
skids and skites from the neck of a bottle
that might turn on him, might turn and sever
an artery, the big one that runs through his wrist.

ELVIS COSTELLO AND THE ATTRACTIONS:
My Aim Is True

Even the *reductio ad absurdum*
of the *quid pro quo* or 'tit for tat'
killing (For 'Eilis' read 'Alison')

that now took over from the street riot
was not without an old-fashioned
sense of decorum, an unseemly seemliness.

WARREN ZEVON: *Excitable Boy*

Somewhere between *Ocean Boulevard* and *Slowhand*
I seemed to have misplaced my wedding band
and taken up with waitresses and usherettes
who drank straight gins and smoked crooked cheroots.

Since those were still the days when more meant less
Georgie was herself playing fast and loose
with the werewolf who, not so very long before,
had come how-howling round our kitchen door

and introduced me to Warren Zevon, whose hymns
to booty, to beasts, to bimbos, boom boom,
are inextricably part of the warp and woof
of the wild and wicked poems in *Quoof*.

There was that time the archangel ran his thumb along
   the shelf
and anointed, it seemed, his own brow with soot.

BLONDIE: *Parallel Lines*

It had taken all morning to rehearse
a tracking shot

with an Arriflex
mounted on a gurney.

The dream of rain
on the face of a well.

'Ready when you are, Mr DeMilledoon.'
Another small crowd

on the horizon.
We should have rented a Steadicam.

So it was I gave up the Oona for the Susquehanna,
the Shannon for the Shenandoah.

Though not before I'd done my stint on the Cam.
The ceilings taller than the horizon.

The in-crowd
on the outs with the likes of Milton

and Spenser while Cromwell
still walked through the pouring rain.

In graveyards from Urney
to Ardglass, my countrymen laying down some *Lex*

talionis: 'Only the guy who's shot
gets to ride in the back of the hearse.'

You can take the man out of Armagh but, you may ask
   yourself,
can you take the Armagh out of the man in the big
   Armani suit?

u2: *The Joshua Tree*

When I went to hear them in Giants Stadium
a year or two ago, the whiff
of kief
brought back the night we drove all night from Palm

Springs to Blythe. No Irish lad and his lass
were so happy as we who roared
and soared
through yucca-scented air. Dawn brought a sense of
  loss,

faint at first, that would deepen and expand
as our own golden chariot
was showered
with Zippo-spears from the upper tiers of the stands.

PINK FLOYD: *A Momentary Lapse of Reason*

We stopped in at a roadhouse on the way back from
   Lyonesse
and ordered a Tom Collins and an Old-Fashioned.
As we remounted the chariot

the poplars' synthesized alamo-alamo-eleison
was counterpointed by a red-headed woodpecker's rat-
   tat-tat
on a snare, a kettledrum's de dum de dum.

PAUL SIMON: *Negotiations and Love Songs*

Little did I think as I knelt by a pot-hole
to water my elephant with the other elephant drivers,
little did I think as I chewed on some betel

that I might one day be following the river
down the West Side Highway in his smoke-glassed
limo complete with bodyguard-cum-chauffeur

and telling him that his lyrics must surely last:
little did I think as I chewed and chewed
that my own teeth and tongue would be eaten by rust.

When I turn up the rickety old gramophone
the wow and flutter from a scratched LP
summons up white walls, the table, the single bed

where Lydia Languish will meet her Le Fanu:
his songs have meant far more to me
than most of the so-called 'poems' I've read.

NIRVANA: *Bleach*

I went there, too, with Mona, or Monica.
Another shot of Absolut.

'The Wild Rover' or some folk anthem
on the jukebox. Some dour

bartender. I, too, have been held fast
by those snares and nets

off the Zinc Coast, the coast of Zanzibar,
                              lost

                    able
                    addiction

             'chin-chins'
                              loos,

'And it's no,
nay, never, no never no more...'

All great artists are their own greatest threat,
as when they aim an industrial laser
at themselves and cut themselves back to the root

so that, with spring, we can never ever be sure
if they shake from head to foot
from an orgasm, you see, sir, or a seizure.

R.E.M.: *Automatic for the People*

Like the grasping for air by an almighty mite
who's suffering from a bad case of the colic.

THE ROLLING STONES: *Voodoo Lounge*

Giants Stadium again ... Again the scent of drugs
struggling through rain so heavy some young Turks
would feel obliged to butt-hole
surf across those vast puddles

on the field. Some might have burned damp faggots
on a night like this, others faked
the ho-ho-hosannas and the hallelujahs
with their *'Tout passe, tout casse, tout lasse.'*

The Stones, of course, have always found the way
of setting a burning brand
to a petrol-soaked stack of hay

and making a 'Thou Shalt'
of a 'Thou Shalt Not'. The sky over the Meadowlands
was still aglow as I drove home to my wife and child.

Hay

This much I know. Just as I'm about to make that right
   turn
off Province Line Road
I meet another beat-up Volvo
carrying a load

of hay. (More accurately, a bale of lucerne
on the roof rack,
a bale of lucerne or fescue or alfalfa.)
My hands are raw. I'm itching to cut the twine, to
   unpack

that hay-accordion, that hay-concertina.
It must be ten o'clock. There's still enough light
(not least from the glow

of the bales themselves) for a body to ascertain
that when one bursts, as now, something takes flight
from those hot and heavy box-pleats. This much, at
   least, I know.

Apple Slump

The bounty-threat of snow
in October. Our apple mound
some boxer fallen foul
of a right swing

waiting for his second to throw –
the sound, turn up the sound –
that mean little towel
into the ring.

The Train

I've been trying, my darling, to explain
to myself how it is that some freight train
loaded with ballast so a track may rest
easier in its bed should be what's roused

us both from ours, tonight as every night,
despite its being miles off and despite
our custom of putting to the very
back of the mind all that's customary

and then, since it takes forever to pass
with its car after car of coal and gas
and salt and wheat and rails and railway ties,

how it seems determined to give the lie
to the notion, my darling,
that we, not it, might be the constant thing.

Three Deer, Mount Rose, August 1995

How about that? As I stepped outside, the doe and her
    twin fawns
stopped midway across the yard. They were so laid-
    back. So serene.
This insouciance might have been enough to evince
their reputation for popping nitroglycerin

to keep their heart-rates steady, had we not known
    already from the mounds
of coffee beans that caffeine is their drug of choice.
Not only were they strung-out on caffeine but Oscar
    MacOscair, the hound
whose name means 'deer-favorite', now favored giving
    chase.

The doe and one fawn got away. The other he caught by
    a bakelite
hock as it knocked its head against chicken wire. The
    Pleiades
had fallen higgledy-piggledy
along its back. All heat of the moment. I could tell from
    its bleats

this black-tongued fawn wanted to free itself, to make a
    clean breast
of something, to blurt
out something to the effect, perhaps, that these were the
    Perseids
rather than the Pleiades, to blurt it out like a Polaroid.

Hopewell Haiku

I

The door of the shed
open-shuts with the clangor
of red against red.

II

A muddle of mice.
Their shit looks like caraway
but smells like allspice.

III

From whin-bright Cave Hill
a blackbird might ... *will* give thanks
with his whin-bright bill.

IV

For now, we must make
do with a thumb-blowing owl
across the fire-break.

V

A stone at its core,
this snowball's the porcelain
knob on winter's door.

VI

Our wild cat, Pangur,
spent last night under the hood
of my old banger.

VII

I tamped it with hay,
the boot that began to leak
Thursday or Friday.

VIII

Snow up to my shanks.
I glance back. The path I've hacked
is a white turf-bank.

IX

Cheek-to-cheek-by-jowl,
from the side of the kettle
my ancestors scowl.

X

A crocus piss-stain.
'There's too much snow in my life,'
my daughter complains.

XI

Pennons in pine woods
where the white-tailed stag and doe
until just now stood.

XII

For most of a week
we've lived on a pot of broth
made from a pig's cheek.

XIII

Burst pipes. Solder-flak.
Now she sports a copper ring
with a hairline crack.

XIV

Though cast in metal,
our doorstop hare finds no place
in which to settle.

XV

The changeless penknife.
The board. The heavy trestles.
The changeless penknife.

XVI

Teasel, that lies low,
aspires to raising the nap
on your woollen throw.

XVII

The finer the cloth
in your *obi*, or waist piece,
the finer the moth.

XVIII

The first day of spring.
What to make of that bald patch
right under the swing?

XIX

A mare's long white face.
A blazed tree marking a trail
we'll never retrace.

XX

The razzle-dazzle
of a pair of Ratatosks
on their Yggdrasill.

XXI

Jean stoops to the tap
set into a maple's groin
for the rising sap.

XXII

The Canada geese
straighten a pantyhose seam,
press a trouser crease.

XXIII

When I set a match
to straw – Whiteboys, Bootashees,
pikestaffs in the thatch.

XXIV

From the white-hot bales
Caravats and Shanavests
step with white-hot flails.

XXV

A hammock at dusk.
I scrimshaw a narwhal hunt
on a narwhal tusk.

XXVI

I, too, nailed a coin
to the mast of the *Pequod*.
A tiny pine cone.

XXVII

The yard's three lonesome
pines are hung with such tokens.
A play by Zeami.

XXVIII

Good Friday. At three,
a swarm of bees sets its heart
on an apple tree.

XXIX

While the goldfinch nest
in the peach tree's eye-level
with a stallion's crest.

XXX

That peach bears the brunt
of the attacks by mildew,
black rot, smuts and bunts.

XXXI

Twilight. Pyewacket
ambles along the ridge-pole
with a tar-bucket.

XXXII

We buy flour, bacon
and beans with pollen we pan
here in the Yukon.

XXXIII

The wide boulevard
where a window-shopping deer
goes by fits and starts.

XXXIV

None more dishevelled
than those who seemed most demure.
Our ragweed-revels.

XXXV

Raspberries. Red-blue.
A paper-cut on the tongue
from a billet-doux.

XXXVI

Now the star-nosed mole
looks back down his long tunnel.
I scrape my boot-soles.

XXXVII

The bold Pangur Ban
draws and quarters a wood thrush
by the garbage can.

XXXVIII

It seems from this sheer
clapboard, fungus-flanged, that walls
do indeed have ears.

XXXIX

A worm for a lure.
The small-mouthed black bass recoil
from my overtures.

XL

Had the thrush not flung
itself at the gin and lime.
Had the trap not sprung.

XLI

Jean paints one toenail.
In a fork of the white ash,
quick, a cardinal.

XLII

Nowadays I flush
a long-drawn-out cry, at most,
from the underbrush.

XLIII

A giant puffball.
The swelled, head-hunted, swelled head
of a king of Gaul.

XLIV

A Saharan boil.
Oscar stretched under a hide
by the toilet bowl.

XLV

There's a trail of slime
that runs from the ladysmock.
I'll show you sometime.

XLVI

At my birthday bash,
a yellow bin for bottles
and a green for trash.

XLVII

Sunflower with fence-posts.
Communion rail. Crozier. Cope.
The monstrance. The host.

XLVIII

From under the shed
a stench that's beyond belief.
Pangur Ban is dead.

XLIX

I lean to one side
to let a funeral pass.
It leans to one side.

L

Now I must take stock.
The ax I swaggered and swung's
split the chopping-block.

LI

In a slow puddle
two dragonflies, Oxford blues,
rest on their paddles.

LII

Saturday night. Soap.
Ametas and Thestylis
still making hay-ropes.

LIII

A ladysmock-thief's
made off with five pairs of smalls
and two handkerchiefs.

LIV

An airplane, alas,
is more likely than thunder
to trouble your glass.

LV

On the highest rung
of my two-pointed ladder
a splash of bird dung.

LVI

Immediately you
tap that old bell of millet
it somehow rings true.

LVII

While from the thistles
that attend our middle age
a goldfinch whistles.

LVIII

A small, hard pear falls
and hits the deck with a thud.
Ripeness is not all.

LIX

Wonder of wonders.
The plow that stood in the hay's
itself plowed under.

LX

Take off his halter
and a horse will genuflect
at a horse-altar.

LXI

Bivouac. Billet.
The moon a waning of lard
on a hot skillet.

LXII

For I wrote this page
by the spasm ... The spasm ...
A firefly ... A cage.

LXIII

The boiler room floods.
Old apple trees lagged with moss.
Live coals in the mud.

LXIV

It's as if he plays
harmonica, the raccoon
with an ear of maize.

LXV

No time since we checked
our scythe blades, our reaping hooks
that are now rust-flecked.

LXVI

Two trees in the yard
bring neither shade nor shelter
but rain, twice as hard.

LXVII

A bullfrog sumo
stares into his bowl of wine.
Those years in Suma.

LXVIII

Now he swims across
a swimming pool. His breast-stroke
leaves me at a loss.

LXIX

Such sallies and swoons.
A starling flock. A total
eclipse of the moon.

LXX

Beyond the corn-stooks
the maples' firewood-detail.
Their little red books.

LXXI

A sudden swelter.
A furnace door throwing light
on the ore smelters.

LXXII

Like a wayside shrine
to itself, this side-swiped stag
of the seven tines.

LXXIII

The leaves of the oak
were boons on a hero's booth.
They've gone up in smoke.

LXXIV

Night. The citadel
gives off carbolic and bleach.
Jeyes' Fluid. Dettol.

LXXV

I've upset the pail
in which my daughter had kept
her five – 'No, *six*' – snails.

LXXVI

And her home-made kite
of less than perfect design?
Also taken flight.

LXXVII

Is that body bag
Cuchulainn's or Ferdia's?
Let's check the dog tag.

LXXVIII

Fresh snow on the roof
of a car that passed me by.
The print of one hoof.

LXXIX

Though the cankered peach
is felled, the bird's nest it held
is still out of reach.

LXXX

That stag I side-swiped.
I watched a last tear run down
his tear duct. I wept.

LXXXI

There's such a fine line
between freezing rain and sleet.
The stag's narrow chine.

LXXXII

A horse farts and farts
on the wind-tormented scarp.
A virtuoso.

LXXXIII

A sang-de-boeuf sky
reflected in a cold-frame
gives the earth the lie.

LXXXIV

The old stag that belled
all night long, tail-end of rut.
How my own heart swelled.

LXXXV

On the road to town
a raccoon in party mask.
Gray shawl. Gray ballgown.

LXXXVI

Winter time, my sweet.
The puppy under our bed
licking salt-raw feet.

LXXXVII

Not a golden carp
but a dog turd under ice.
Not a golden carp.

LXXXVIII

That wavering flame
is the burn-off from a mill.
Star of Bethlehem.

LXXXIX

Fishermen have cut
a hole in the frozen lake.
No smoke from their hut.

XC

The maple's great cask
that once held so much in store
now yields a hip flask.

Anonymous: *Myself and Pangur*

Myself and Pangur, my white cat,
have much the same calling, in that
much as Pangur goes after mice
I go hunting for the precise

word. He and I are much the same
in that I'm gladly 'lost to fame'
when on the *Georgics*, say, I'm bent
while he seems perfectly content

with his lot. Life in the cloister
can't possibly lose its lustre
so long as there's some crucial point
with which we might by leaps and bounds

yet grapple, into which yet sink
our teeth. The bold Pangur will think
through mouse-snagging much as I muse
on something naggingly abstruse,

then fix his clear, unflinching eye
on our lime-white cell wall, while I
focus, in so far as I can,
on the limits of what a man

may know. Something of his rapture
at his most recent mouse-capture
I share when I, too, get to grips
with what has given me the slip.

And so we while away our whiles,
never cramping each other's styles
but practicing the noble arts
that so lift and lighten our hearts,

Pangur going in for the kill
with all his customary skill
while I, sharp-witted, swift and sure,
shed light on what had seemed obscure.

Rainer Maria Rilke: *Black Cat*

Despite its being invisible, a ghost has enough mass
to take your glance and give it glancingly back;
here, though, your sternest look will pass
not through but *into* her fur, fur as dense and black
as the walls against which a madman pounds
his fists, the padded
cell against which, all night long, he expends
himself until his fury has abated.
For it seems that she has somehow been able to keep
within herself every glance that's ever been cast
at her as, bristling, up for battle,
she gives them the once-over before falling asleep.
Then, as if starting from slumber,
she turns her face directly towards your own
and you see yourself, held fast
in the yellow stone
of her eye like a bug, like a long-extinct beetle
set in a lump of amber.

Paunch

Barefoot, in burgundy shorts and a salmon-pink
T-shirt, I pad across the deck
and sink
into one of four old Adirondack

chairs that themselves slump into themselves. There's a
    flare
from the citronella bucket
as, there,
our eight-week-old stray kitten, Pyewacket,

ventures across what might have seemed a great divide
between her and me, had she not
now begun to nag and needle

and knead
my paunch for milk. The bucket fills with human fat.
The chair takes a dim view through a knot-hole.

Long Finish

Ten years since we were married, since we stood
under a chuppah of pine boughs
in the middle of a little pinewood
and exchanged our wedding vows.
Save me, good thou,
a piece of marchpane, while I fill your glass with Simi
Chardonnay as high as decency allows,
and then some.

Bear with me now as I myself must bear
the scrutiny of a bottle of wine
that boasts of hints of plum and pear,
its muscadine
tempered by an oak backbone. I myself have designs
on the willow-boss
of your breast, on all your waist confines
between longing and loss.

The wonder is that we somehow have withstood
the soars and slumps in the Dow
of ten years of marriage and parenthood,
its summits and its sloughs –
that we've somehow
managed to withstand an almond-blossomy
five years of bitter rapture, five of blissful rows
(and then some,

if we count the one or two to spare
when we've been firmly on cloud nine).
Even now, as you turn away from me with your one
    bare
shoulder, the veer of your neckline,
I glimpse the all-but-cleared-up eczema patch on your
    spine
and it brings to mind not the Schloss
that stands, transitory, tra la, Triestine,
between longing and loss

but a crude
hip-trench in a field, covered with pine boughs,
in which two men in masks and hoods
who have themselves taken vows
wait for a farmer to break a bale for his cows
before opening fire with semi-
automatics, cutting him off slightly above the eyebrows,
and then some.

It brings to mind another, driving out to care
for six white-faced kine
finishing on heather and mountain air,
another who'll shortly divine
the precise whereabouts of a landmine
on the road between Beragh and Sixmilecross,
who'll shortly know what it is to have breasted the line
between longing and loss.

Such forbearance in the face of vicissitude
also brings to mind the little 'there, there's and 'now,
    now's
of two sisters whose sleeves are imbued
with the constant douse and souse
of salt-water through their salt-house
in *Matsukaze* (or 'Pining Wind'), by Zeami,
the salt-house through which the wind soughs and
    soughs,
and then some

of the wind's little 'now, now's and 'there, there's
seem to intertwine
with those of Pining Wind and Autumn Rain, who must
    forbear
the dolor of their lives of boiling down brine.
For the double meaning of 'pine'
is much the same in Japanese as English, coming across
both in the sense of 'tree' and the sense we assign
between 'longing' and 'loss'

as when the ghost of Yukihira, the poet-courtier who
    wooed
both sisters, appears as a ghostly pine, pining among
    pine boughs.
Barely have Autumn Rain and Pining Wind renewed
their vows
than you turn back towards me and your blouse,
while it covers the all-but-cleared-up patch of eczema,
falls as low as decency allows,
and then some.

Princess of Accutane, let's no more try to refine
the pure drop from the dross
than distinguish, good thou, between mine and thine,
between longing and loss,
but rouse
ourselves each dawn, here on the shore at Suma,
with such force and fervor as spouses may yet espouse,
and then some.

The Throwback

Even I can't help but notice, my sweet,
that when you tuck your chin
into your chest, as if folding a sheet
while holding a clothes-pin

between your teeth, or when, a small detail,
you put your hands like so
on your little pot-belly and twiddle
your thumbs like so, it's as if you're a throw-

back to the grandmother you never met,
the mother whom I sight
in this reddish patch of psoriasis

behind your ear that might
suddenly flare up into the helmet
she wore when she stood firm against Xerxes.

They that Wash on Thursday

She was such a dab hand, my mother. Such a dab hand
at raising her hand
to a child. At bringing a cane down across my hand
in such a seemingly off-hand
manner I almost have to hand
it to her. 'Many hands,'
she would say, 'spoil the broth.' My father took no hand
in this. He washed his hands
of the matter. He sat on his hands.
So I learned first hand
to deal in the off-, the under-, the sleight-of-hand,
writing now in that great, open hand
yet never quite showing my hand.
I poured myself a drink with a heavy hand.
As for the women with whom I sat hand in hand
in the Four in Hand,
as soon as they were eating out of my hand
I dismissed them out of hand.
Then one would play into my hands –
or did she force my hand? –
whose lily-white hand
I took in marriage. I should have known beforehand
it wouldn't work. 'When will you ever take yourself in
    hand?'
'And give you the upper hand?'
For things were by now completely out of hand.
The show of hands
on a moonlit hill under the Red Hand.
The Armalite in one hand

and the ballot box in the other. Men dying at hand.
Throughout all of which I would hand
back to continuity as the second hand
came up to noon. 'On the one hand . . .
On the other . . .' The much-vaunted even hand
of the BBC. Though they'd pretty much given me a free
   hand
I decided at length to throw in my hand
and tendered my resignation 'by hand'.
I was now quite reconciled to living from hand
to mouth. (Give that man a big, big hand.)
My father was gone. My mother long gone. Into Thy
   hands,
O Lord . . . Gone, too, the ink-stained hands
of Mary Powers. Now I'd taken another lily-white hand
put in by the hole of the door. A hand
no bigger than a cloud. Now she and I and the child of
   my right hand
stand hand in hand,
brave Americans all, and I know ('The bird in the hand
is the early bird . . .') that the time is at hand
for me to set my hand
to my daughter's still-wet, freehand
version of the Muldoon 'coat of arms' that came to hand
in a heraldry shop on Nassau Street – on a green field a
   white hand.

Blissom

The thing is, when Agnieszka and I lay like bride and
   groom
in the refuse-tip
of her six-by-eight-by-six-foot bed-sitting-room

I awoke as a Prince of Serendip
between her legs,
given how my mind would skip

from pegs to kegs to tegelmousted Tuaregs
while I peered through the skylight as if from an open
   tomb
at those five ewe- and three wether-tegs.

The Little Black Book

It was Aisling who first soft-talked my penis-tip
   between her legs
while teasing open that Velcro strip between her legs.

Cliona, then. A skinny country girl.
The small stream, in which I would skinny-dip,
   between her legs.

Born and bred in Londinium, the stand-offish Etain,
who kept a stiff upper lip between her legs.

Grainne. Grain goddess. The last, triangular shock of
   corn,
through which a sickle might rip, between her legs.

Again and again that winter I made a bee-line for Ita,
for the sugar-water sip between her legs.

The spring brought not only Liadan but her memory of
   Cuirithir,
his ghostly one-up-manship between her legs.

(Ita is not to be confused with her steely half-sister,
   Niamh,
she of the ferruginous drip between her legs.)

It was Niamh, as luck would have it, who introduced
   me to Orla.
The lost weekend of a day trip between *her* legs.

It was Orla, as luck would have it, who introduced me
    to Roisin.
The bramble-patch. The rosehip between her legs.

What ever became of Sile?
Sile who led me to horse-worship between her legs.

As for Janet from the Shankill, who sometimes went by
    'Sinead',
I practiced my double back-flip between her legs.

I had a one-on-one tutorial with Siobhan.
I read *The Singapore Grip* between her legs.

And what ever became of Sorcha, Sorcha, Sorcha?
Her weakness for the whip between her legs.

Or the big-boned, broad-shouldered Treasa?
She asked me to give her a buzzclip between her legs.

Or the little black sheep, Una, who kept her own little
    black book?
I fluttered, like an erratum slip, between her legs.

Errata

For 'Antrim' read 'Armagh'.
For 'mother' read 'other'.
For 'harm' read 'farm'.
For 'feather' read 'father'.

For 'Moncrieff' read 'Monteith'.
For *'Béal Fierste'* read *'Béal Feirste'*.
For 'brave' read 'grave'.
For 'revered' read 'reversed'.

For 'married' read 'marred'.
For 'pull' read 'pall'.
For 'ban' read 'bar'.
For 'smell' read 'small'.

For 'spike' read 'spoke'.
For 'lost' read 'last'.
For 'Steinbeck' read 'Steenbeck'.
For 'ludic' read 'lucid'.

For 'religion' read 'region'.
For 'ode' read 'code'.
For 'Jane' read 'Jean'.
For 'rod' read 'road'.

For 'pharoah' read 'pharaoh'.
For *'Fíor-Gael'* read *'Fíor-Ghael'*.
For 'Jeffrey' read 'Jeffery'.
For 'vigil' read 'Virgil'.

For 'flageolet' read 'fava'.
For 'veto' read 'vote'.
For 'Aiofe' read 'Aoife'.
For 'anecdote' read 'antidote'.

For 'Rosemont' read 'Mount Rose'.
For 'plump' read 'plumb'.
For 'hearse' read 'hears'.
For 'loom' read 'bloom'.

Horses

I

A sky. A field. A hedge flagrant with gorse.
I'm trying to remember, as best I can,
if I'm a man dreaming I'm a plowhorse
or a great plowhorse dreaming I'm a man.

II

Midsummer Eve. St John's wort. Spleenwort. Spurge.
I'm hard on the heels of the sage, Chuang Tzu,
when he slips into what was once a forge
through a door in the shape of a horseshoe.

A Journey to Cracow

As we high-tailed it across the meadows
towards what might have been common ground
we were dragged down by our own shadows
through a dance-floor near Wanda's mound

towards what might have been. Common ground?
Only when a black horse plunges
through a dance-floor near Wanda's mound
do they take the barn door off its hinges,

only when a black horse plunges
into the Vistula swollen with rain
do they take the barn door off its hinges
to beat out the black grain.

Into the Vistula swollen with rain
you and I might have plunged and found a way
to beat out the black grain
as our forefathers did on threshing day,

you and I might have plunged and found a way
to set a cigarette on the barn door
as our forefathers did on threshing day
and dance rings around it for evermore,

to set a cigarette on the barn door
wherever it might be, for an instant, even
and dance rings around it for evermore
in some polka or Cracovienne,

whatever that might be. For an instant, even
we were dragged down by our own shadows,
my love, in some polka or mazurka or Cracovienne
as we high-tailed it across the meadows.

Aftermath

I

'Let us now drink,' I imagine patriot cry to patriot
after they've shot
a neighbor in his own aftermath, who hangs still
    between two sheaves
like Christ between two tousle-headed thieves,
his body wired up to the moon, as like as not.

II

To the memory of another left to rot
near some remote beauty spot,
the skin of his right arm rolled up like a shirtsleeve,
let us now drink.

III

Only a few nights ago, it seems, they set fire to a big
    house and it got
so preternaturally hot
we knew there would be no reprieve
till the swallows' nests under the eaves
had been baked into these exquisitely glazed little pots
from which, my love, let us now drink.

Wire

As I roved out this morning at daybreak
I took a short cut
through the pine forest, following the high-tension wires
past the timber line
till I stumbled upon a makeshift hide or shooting-box
from which a command-wire seemed to run

intermittently along the ski-run
or fire-break.
I glanced into the hideout. A school lunch-box.
A pear so recently cut
I thought of Ceylon. A can of Valvoline.
Crocodile clips. Sri Lanka, I mean. A hank of wire

that might come in handy if ever I'd want to hot-wire
a motor and make a run
for the border. From just beyond my line
of vision I glimpsed something, or someone, break
cover for an instant. A shaved head, maybe, or a crew-
    cut.
Jumping up like a jack-in-the-box

before ducking back down. Then a distant raking
    through the gear-box
of a truck suddenly gone haywire
on this hillside of hillsides in Connecticut
brought back some truck on a bomb run,
brought back so much with which I'd hoped to break –
the hard-line

yet again refusing to toe the line,
the bullet and the ballot box,
the joy-ride, the jail-break,
Janet endlessly singing 'The Men behind the Wire',
the endless re-run
of Smithfield, La Mon, Enniskillen, of bodies cut

to ribbons as I heard the truck engine cut
and, you might have read as much between the lines,
ducked down here myself behind the hide. As if I myself
    were on the run.
The truck driver handing a box-
cutter, I'm sure, to the bald guy. A pair of real live
    wires.
I've listened to them all day now, torn between making
    a break

for it and their talk of the long run, the short term, of
    boxing clever,
fish or cut bait, make or break,
the end of the line, right down to the wire.

Rune

What can I tell you? Though your quarry
lies exhausted at the bottom of an exhausted quarry,

to follow that lure
will almost certainly end in failure.

While I did indeed sink
like a stone among bottles, cans, a fridge, a sink,

a slab of marble, granite
or slate I'm not. By the window of an All-Nite

Café or a 24-Hour Bank
I, too, stretched as if on a flowery bank

and admired
my shiny, former self, a self even then mired

in the idea that what you saw
was what you got.

Why would a hostage's hand hacked off with a hacksaw
weigh on me now like a blood-spattered ingot

from that 24-Hour Bank, I who once cut such a figure
in its drive-up window? Go figure.

Third Epistle to Timothy

You made some mistake when you intended to favor me with
some of the new valuable grass seed ... for what you gave me
... proves mere timothy.

A letter from Benjamin Franklin to Jared Eliot,
July 16th, 1747

I

Midnight. June, 1923. Not a stir except for the brough
     and brouhaha
surrounding the taper or link
in which a louse
flares up and a shadow, my da's,
clatters against a wall of the six-by-eight-by-six-foot
     room
he sleeps in, eleven years old, a servant-boy at Hardy's
     of Carnteel.
There's a boot-polish lid filled with turps
or paraffin oil
under each cast-iron bed-leg, a little barrier
against bed-bugs under each bed-foot.

II

That knocking's the knocking against their stalls of a
     team
of six black Clydesdales mined in Coalisland
he's only just helped to unhitch from the cumbersome
star of a hay-rake. Decently and in order
he brought each whitewashed nose
to its nosebag of corn, to its galvanized bucket.
One of the six black Clydesdale mares

he helped all day to hitch and unhitch
was showing, on the near hock, what might be a bud of
    farcy
picked up, no doubt, while on loan to Wesley Cummins.

III

'Decently and in order,' Cummins would proclaim, 'let
    all Inniskillings
be done.' A week ago my da helped him limber up
the team to a mowing machine as if to a gun carriage.
    'For no Dragoon
can function without his measure of char.'
He patted his belly-band. 'A measure, that is, against
    dysentery.'
This was my da's signal to rush
into the deep shade of the hedge to fetch such little tea
    as might remain
in the tea urn. 'Man does not live,' Cummins would
    snort, 'only by scraps
of wheaten farls and tea dregs.
You watch your step or I'll see you're shipped back to
    Killeter.'

IV

'Killeeshill,' my da says, 'I'm from Killeeshill.' Along
    the cast-iron
rainbow of his bed-end
comes a line
of chafers or cheeselips that have scaled the bed-legs
despite the boot-polish lids. Eleven years of age. A
    servant-boy

on the point of falling asleep. The reek of paraffin
or the pinewoods reek
of turpentine
good against roundworm in horses. That knocking
   against their stalls
of six Clydesdales, each standing at sixteen hands.

V

Building hay even now, even now drawing level with
   the team's head-brass,
buoyed up by nothing more than the ballast
of hay – meadow cat's-tail, lucerne, the leaf upon
   trodden leaf
of white clover and red–
drawing level now with the taper-blooms of a horse
   chestnut.
Already light in the head.
'Though you speak, young Muldoon...' Cummins calls
   up from trimming the skirt
of the haycock, 'though you speak with the tongue
of an angel, I see you for what you are ... Malevolent.
Not only a member of the church malignant but a
   malevolent spirit.'

VI

Even now borne aloft by bearing down on lap-cocks and
   shake-cocks
from under one of which a ruddy face
suddenly twists and turns upwards as if itself carried
on a pitchfork and, meeting its gaze,
he sees himself, a servant-boy still, still ten or eleven,

breathing upon a Clydesdale's near hock and finding a
    farcy-bud
like a tiny glow in a strut of charcoal.
'I see you,' Cummins points at him with the pitchfork,
    'you little by-blow,
I see you casting your spells, your sorceries,
I see you coming as a thief in the night to stab us in the
    back.'

VII

A year since they kidnapped Anketell Moutray from his
    home at Favour Royal,
dragging him, blindfolded, the length of his own gravel
    path,
eighty years old, the Orange county grand master. Four
    A-Specials shot on a train
in Clones. The Clogher valley
a blaze of flax-mills and hay-sheds. Memories of the
    Land League. Davitt and Biggar.
Breaking the boycott at Lough Mask.
The Land Leaguers beaten
at the second battle of Saintfield. It shall be revealed...
A year since they cut out the clapper of a collabor ... a
    collabor...
a collaborator from Maguiresbridge.

VIII

That knocking's the team's near-distant knocking on wood
while my da breathes upon
the blue-yellow flame on a fetlock, on a deep-feathered
    pastern

of one of six black Shires ... 'Because it shall be
  revealed by fire,'
Cummins's last pitchfork is laden
with thistles, 'as the sparks fly upward
man is born unto trouble. For the tongue may yet be cut
from an angel.' The line of cheeselips and chafers
along the bed-end. 'Just wait till you come back down
  and I get a hold
of you, young Muldoon ... We'll see what spells you'll
  cast.'

IX

For an instant it seems no one else might scale
such a parapet of meadow cat's-tail, lucerne, red and
  white clovers,
not even the line of chafers and cheeselips
that overthrow as they undermine
when, light in the head, unsteady on his pegs as
  Anketell Moutray,
he squints through a blindfold of clegs
from his grass-capped, thistle-strewn vantage point,
the point where two hay-ropes cross,
where Cummins and his crew have left him, in a straw
  hat with a fraying brim,
while they've moved on to mark out the next haycock.

X

That next haycock already summoning itself from
  windrow after wind-weary windrow
while yet another brings itself to mind in the acrid stink
of turpentine. There the image of Lizzie,

Hardy's last servant-girl, reaches out from her dais
of salt hay, stretches out an unsunburned arm
half in bestowal, half beseechingly, then turns away to
    appeal
to all that spirit-troop
of hay-treaders as far as the eye can see, the coil on coil
of hay from which, in the taper's mild uproar,
they float out across the dark face of the earth, an earth
    without form, and void.

A Half-Door near Cluny

```
s t a b l e s t a b l e s t a b l e s
t a b l e s t a b l e s t a b l e s t
a b l e s t a b l e s t a b l e s t a
b l e s                     s t a b
l e s t                     t a b l
e s t a                     a b l e
s t a b                     b l e s
t a b l         b l é       l e s t
a b l e                     e s t a
b l e s                     s t a b
l e s t                     t a b l
e s t a                     a b l e
s t a b l e s t a b l e s t a b l e s
t a b l e s t a b l e s t a b l e s t
a b l e s t a b l e s t a b l e s t a
b l e s t a b l e s t a b l e s t a b
l e s t a b l e s t a b l e s t a b l
e s t a b l e s t a b l e s t a b l e
s t a b l e s t a b l e s t a b l e s
```

Burma

In memory of Charles Monteith

Thunder and lightning. The veil of the temple rent
in twain
as I glimpse through the flackering flap of the tent
the rain

flash-flooding across the shoulders and roughed-out head
of one
of sixteen elephants – putty-colored, teak-red,
blue, dun –

that now skip round the ring to flourish their blunt
   tusks,
their capes
of rain-dark jute or sisal or coconut husks,

to foist
themselves upon the public, one day to escape
the pavilion which, this morning, we watched them
   hoist.

The Hug
In memory of Joseph Brodsky

'Of course, of course, of course,' I heard you intone
in your great peaches-and-diesel tenor
as I drew up to the airport in Cologne,
'there's an Auden in every Adenauer

though politicians and poets embrace, you see,
only before a masque or after a massacre.'
We sat with our daughters on our knees.
'Poets and politicians are close ... but no Cigar.'

You would break the filter tip off a Camel –
'They're infinitely better "circumcised" ' –
and pour another Absolut, *du lieber Himmel*,
eschewing absolutely the lemon zest.

You had such gusto, Joseph: for an afternoon trip
to the hallowed ground of Middagh Street;
dim sum in Soho, all those bits and bobs of tripe
and chickens' gizzards and chickens' feet

and dumplings filled with gristle
that reminded you of the labor camp
near Archangel. As I left the church of Saint Ursula
yesterday afternoon, I was already quite overcome

by the walls of *die Goldene Kammer*
swagged with human bones, already quite taken aback
by its abecedary, its Latin grammar,
of fibulas and femurs, its rack

of shanks and shoulderblades,
when a blast of air from, I guess, the Caucasus
threw its arms around me in the Ursulaplatz
with what was surely your 'Kisses, kisses, kisses.'

White

In memory of Thaddeus Wills (June 19th – June 20th, 1996)

Your mother shows me a photograph of you got up in
   lace.
White crêpe-de-chine. White bonnet. White mittens.
Once, on a street in Moscow, a woman pushed snow in
   my face
when it seemed I might have been frost-bitten.

The Fridge

An ogham stone stands four-square as the fridge
I open yet again to forage
for a bottle of Smithwicks or Bass
when '*Beárrthóir* means "a barber",' O'Boyle avers,
'but *bearradóir* in Gortahork
is "a cow that eats at other cows' tails..."'
and there's a faint whiff of a chemistry lab

as through the fridge door there pass
three old teachers, three philosophers
who followed the narrow track
to the highest good, followed a cattle trail
to this four-square limestone slab
with one straight edge all notches and nicks:
Sean O'Boyle; John McCarter; Jerry Hicks.

The Bangle (Slight Return)

If it is true that by death we once more become what we were before being, would it not have been better to abide by that pure possibility, not to stir from it? What use was this detour, when we might have remained forever in an unrealized plenitude?

> E. M. Cioran, *The Trouble with Being Born*
> (translated by Richard Howard)

Does the fetus dream? If so, of what? No one knows.

> Harold M. Schmeck, *New York Times*

CECILY: Uncle Jack is sending you to Australia.

ALGERNON: Australia! I'd sooner die.

CECILY: Well, he said at dinner on Wednesday night, that you would have to choose between this world, the next world, and Australia.

> Oscar Wilde, *The Importance of Being Earnest*

'The beauty of it,' ventured Publius Vergilius Maro,
'is that your father and the other skinnymalinks
may yet end up a pair of jackaroos
in the canefields north of Brisbane.' We heard the tink

of blade on bone, the Greeks' alalaes
as they slashed and burned, saw Aeneas daddle-dade
his father Anchises, and his son, Iulus,
to a hidey-hole on the slopes of Mount Ida.

'The beauty of it is that I delivered them from harm;
it was I who had Aeneas steal
back to look for Creusa, I who had her spirit rub

like a flame through his flame-burnished arms,
I who might have let him find his own way through the
    streel
of smoke, among the cheerless dead, the dying's
    chirrups.'

Even as I felt their death throes in the thrum and throb
of a ship's engine and looked into the roil
of its wake I recognized his suitcase by the strap.
Even as a wind blew up from the Sea of Moyle

to meet a headwind from beyond Stranraer
and those two winds vied
for supremacy in the air
there was a glimmer of something from across the
    divide.

Even as I felt their death throes in the strim and strum
of its engine as the packet rounded a headland
there was a glimmer from across the chasm

that lit his glib all glabrous with Brylcreem,
all brilliantine-brilliant,
that glinted and glittered and gleamed as from Elysium.

A restaurant off the Champs-Elysées. Ray's wing.
  Consommé.
The waiter about to take my dessert order
when there was a cry of *'Bravo'* followed by a
  'Bravissimo'
from the next table but one. Two men. A woman who
  brought back a reporter

I knew in Belfast. A moment's silence in which the men
  tested the nose
('We call it the "nose" rather than the "bouquet"')
of their Hennessys
was broken now by the tink of ice in my ice bucket.

'A demain,' she seemed to pout, *'à demain, mon
  amour...'*
and her bracelet would twitter and twitch
as if to stress the phrase

while, to stress it all the more,
the floor began to roll and pitch
as the headwind from beyond Stranraer reached gale
  force.

Now that the great engine was suddenly thrown into
     reverse
I studied the menu as a catechumen
might his catechism. The *gâteau aux framboises et
     fraises*
or the *gâteau icumen*

in, lhude sing, lhude sing,
as the Châteauneuf-du-Pape
kicked in. The waiter's eyebrow-ring
glittering as he drew himself up

to recommend the *Caprice des Dieux*, his *nu sculon
     herigean*
counterpointed by the jitter and jaunt and jar
of their harness, their own improvised *ceintures*

de ficelle, when my da and that other larrikin
trotted off down the road between Duchess, maybe, and
     Dajarra
to join the rest of the cane-snedders.

v

'The beauty of it,' ventured Virgil, 'is that it was I who
    had the sentries
look the other way so that Creusa might brush
like an incendiary
through your arms, I who gave strong drink to you who
    were ready to perish,

I who had Creusa pout, "*A demain*",
I who had you recognize his cuirass by its strap
as the packet labored against the raging main,
I who had him stand in his stirrups

as he and the other skinnymalinks rode along the track
to the slow clatter
of manganese ore, or zinc, or iron that sharpeneth iron,

I who had you look into the dark
and recognize the glitter
of stars over the mighty Wooroonooran.'

The waiter drew himself up in his full-length white
   empyrean
when he saw me tend
towards another bottle of the Côtes du Rhône,
licked the end

of his pencil, drew a line
and began to catalogue,
with all the little tuts and twitters and whistle-whines
that are the mark of capability and godlike

reason, the damage done by my convoy,
my caravan,
of consommé, salad and ray's wing braked

on a bed of bockchoy,
so I called out to him for a wedge of Bonderay au Foin
and he jabbed his pencil with such force it must surely
   break.

Even now my da and that other jolly swagman would
   rake
their horses over the manganese-bright stones
and into the canebrake.
That streel of smoke. That tink of blade on bone.

The Greeks' al-al-al-al-alalaes
as they fought hand to hand
under the shadow of Troy's smoke-blackened walls.
Until there again, as if wounded, she threw up her right
   hand

and I glanced the glance of one of those kookaburras
through the canebrake, the kookaburra that laughs last,
and I heard her laugh

as I continued to peruse
the dessert-menu-cum-wine-list,
every so often turning over a new coolibar leaf.

Half a love, half a love, half a love, half a love
was better than no bride
as my da bent to unpick the clove-
hitch in the twine with which his manganese-red

suitcase was bound, his tatty-natty
glib falling forward to meet that headwind from beyond in which she unpicked the knot
in her pocket-book, steadied herself against the
  bulkhead

and cupped her hands around a cigarette.
The streel of smoke. The tink and tonk
as the Greeks hastened from tent to tent

in their nightclubbers' boots and short skirts.
The waiter setting his pencil-point on his tongue.
A tongue stud or some such ornament.

Now there came that sweat-and-tobacco scent
as when the spirit
rubs like a flame across the back of a spent
horse that's been spurred

on across the paddocks
to a fence it cannot but refuse.
Now shock after straw-blond shock
would fall across Creusa's face

while I continued to put the little bit of a carte
before the laughing jackass's
'*Au foin? Au foin? Au foin? Au foin?*'

at which moment she looked at me. A look of regret,
already, for what might not be. A gaze
that lasted for a count of five or six. Six or seven.

X

Even as I myself tried to keep myself on an even
keel as if I had indeed been put
drunk into the Newhaven–
Dieppe packet boat

she touched one eye, smudging her kohl,
and turned to watch the traffic flow
towards the Place Charles de Gaulle.
I had been struck no less deadly a blow

by the combination of Australian Syrah
and an intolerable deal of sack
than when, as he and the swagman rode alongside the
    rails,

a cassowary, heh,
stopped my da's cow-pony, ho, in its tracks
and with a razor-sharp middle claw ripped out its
    entrails.

It might have been just then as, cassowarily,
the Greeks made their way through the aftermath
of the battle, their unruly
locks all blood-brilliant from the bloodbath,

as they moved through the smoke-blackened ruins,
thatch smouldering like a black millefeuille,
that a manganese-laden train
clattered down the slopes of Mount Isa and wistfully

the waiter licked his pencil-point. *'Si Monsieur l'épicure
voudrait un petit verre de Muscat*
(I noticed his pants were held up by binder twine)

avec ses bigarreaux?'
There was a silence more awkward than that following
   a miscue
on the next pool table but one.

It seems that my da might have been a little uptight, a
    little *boutonné*,
even as he hurtled through the canefields
on some flea-bitten
cow-pony, even as he hurtled across bogs, fens, flats,

clip-joints and clapiers –
we'll cross that bridge, we'll cross that bridge
when we come to the coolibars
that run along the ridge

of Mount Isa, the coolibars and bloodwoods –
even as she gave me that look so frank, so open,
that she herself was forced to turn

away as a frog he would, a frog he would
like to recommend a little glass of the Beaune
or maybe a little glass of the Sauternes.

XIII

Now the packet thrummed and throbbed from stem to
    stern
as St Elmo's fire
took a turn
along the deck and rigging and the cheese-wire

flashed like a guillotine
from the corner of my eye. Her arm running through a
    terret
of cheesecloth or tarlatan.
Though I knew in my heart of hearts

I should call it quits
something made me want to persevere,
made me want to hold with the hold with the hold

with the Muscadet
de Sèvres de Sèvres de Sèvres
as the flea-bitten pony came to a sudden halt.

XIV

As the packet tried to hold to hold to hold
its course there was a glimmer from the distant coast—
from the Mull of Kintyre or Holyhead—
though the gusts

that reached Force 10 on the Beaufort scale
seemed unlikely to blow over
any time soon and we might have to turn tail
and run for cover

since there's many a slip
twixt what one supposedly determines
and the al-al-al-al-aleatory

where a cow-pony gives up on the slopes
of Mount Isa or the Hay's meanderings come to mean
nothing on the border of Queensland and the Northern
   Territory.

XV

'Si Monsieur l'épicure ... Si Monsieur l'épicure voudrait
un verre de Veuve Clicquot
après son Bonderay
au Foin...?' All the little godlike clucks

and clicketings. His pants
held up by a binder-twine crios.
The pencil-point
on his tongue. *'L'addition, s'il vous plaît.'* While across

the chasm, through the battle-brume,
I could but gawk
at Creusa, could but gape at her prim,

at her prissy-prim
little mouth while too many cooks, while too many
  cooks
made light work of the daughter of Priam.

It was downhill all the way after that. The opprobrium
of the waiter of waiters. To have your cake
and eat bigarroons *and* Bonderay au Foin? His new
  imperium
sweeping clean through the muskeg

in which my da and your man had ridden their cock
horses roughshod over my *crise*
d'un certain âge, my da trying in vain to kick-
start the cow-pony, my calling out 'Creusa, Creusa,
  Creusa'

as the packet reached the midway- and turning-point.
A French edition of *Chaos*. James Gleick.
I'm sure I overheard one of the Hennessys' '*Il est très . . .*

Il a un certain . . . embonpoint.'
Which brought a faint smile to the prim little mouth of
  this lookalike
of a reporter I used to know back in Troy.

That thrum and throb. An engine in reverse. His
   involuntary
clucks and clicketings as the waiter examined
the credit card I must have set on his tray.
A train laden with manganese from the open-cast mine

where, on his first day, the foreman handed him a pink
   slip
which he mulled over,
I see it now, 'Mul-do-on, *non? Avec trois syllabes?*'
Now I would do my best endeavours

in cutting through that Force 10 gale –
'Till May is out,' I wanted to cry, 'ne'er cast
a clout, my duck, for hold-

fast isn't the only horse that for want of a coat of mail
was lost to a hippocaust.'
I watched as the cow-pony watched its own entrails
   unfold.

Downhill all the way as the packet pitched and rolled
and made heavy weather
of a groundswell that seemed as likely to overturn as
   uphold
the established order, such order as we decipher

while we sit and play, or are played by, our toccatas,
stately at the clavichord.
As for my Creusa, as for my little coquette,
though I knew in my heart of hearts

that one night's ice is not a Neapolitan,
hey, knew that I might only aspire
to taking a turn

with her through the Latin
Quarter, ho, I nonetheless appealed to the Mull of
   Kintyre
for the *'keee-yaah'* or *'kikikikik'* of a common tern.

'I make no distinction,' Virgil went on, 'between
  "Trojan" and "Tyrian"
when it comes to the use of weapons
of war...' Now Creusa would somehow happen to turn
the world upside-down just as my da would happen

to untie the not a whit
of the suitcase and shake out a pair of corduroy breeches
rolled up in which was a wad
of newspapers ... 'For it was I who had a Hennessy
  broach

the subject of joining their fellow nightclubbers
on the Avenue des Invalides
so that Creusa might look up ... I make no distinction
  between

that and the collopers
of their own dear flesh who move through the
  battlefield
at the prompting of a bottle of poteen.'

'*Notre ami…*' said the other Hennessy, '*il a une grande
  bedaine…*'
The rest was lost in the groundswell of muzak
and the tough and rumble of half a dozen Bedouin
as she touched one eye, smudging her masc-

ara, a smudge that still beggars
description, the yoicks and yo-hos of half a dozen
  scrofulous
rag- and pocket-pickers
as a crowd of blackfellows ('*Cette carte de crédit est
  volée?*')

gathered around to grab at the reins
of the cow-pony, my da and the other skinnymalinks
  both
staring into the 'unreal-

ized plenitude', both looking back down the drain
of eternity on their enterprise of such great pith…
Heigh ho, says Anthony Rowley.

For 'pith' read 'flight path'. For 'Rowley' read 'Orly'.
When might this throwback
to my reporter from Belfast reel-to-reel
through the blazing town as Aeneas stumbled under the
   weight of Anchises on his back

like a man who's had an intolerable deal of Izarra?
Not even if a low-
flying plane with its leather-capped janissary
were to come through the window in slo-

mo, ho, would her look, so lacking in guile,
waver. 'The beauty of it,' Virgil was saying, 'the sheer
   beauty
of it is not even

that would quell
the blood in her pint pot and have the storm abate
and the sea glitter as it glittered once for Xenophon.'

Even now the wind died down and the heavens
cleared as Creusa stashed away her paperback of *Chaos*.
Where the Hay gave way to the river of oblivion
my da tried to pack the suitcase-numbles back into the
     suitcase,

all but the newspaper sop. 'A gift horse is soon curried,'
Virgil would improvise,
'*mais nous acceptons seulement Mastercard
ou Visa...*'

as one blackfellow drew and fired what looked like a
     pair of matchlocks
into the cow-pony's head. A double spurt
of flame giving vent

to a double spurt of brain from the brain-box.
'*Et votre Amex est, en tout cas* ... expired.'
A twitter-twitch from the cow-pony as it came and
     went.

And from the tangle of its straps and war accoutrements
all clinquant with blood and dung
nothing would seem more eloquent
than the little cow-pony's snaffle-scarred tongue,

snaffle- and sawgrass-scarred,
except perhaps his forelock falling over his forehead
as my da scoured
the classifieds in *The Tyre Courier* and back by
  Holyhead

and the Mull of Kintyre at a rate of knots
the packet steamed as he tried to read
the small print by the Gulf

of Carpentaria and the drain of eternity and the nod
as good as sparing the rod
to a horse looked in the mouth. (See overleaf.)

'For want of an ell the horse changed in mid-life
was lost, as your lovely lass was lost
when she cut her coat according to the cheesecloth
or tarlatan from which there blazed

her titanium vambrace.
You can't make a belly-band
out of a silk purse.
Give them a bird in the hand

and they take not only an ell
but an ell in cretonne
or brocatelle. Your lovely lass adjusting the baldric

of her manganese-red hold-all.
You can't get blood from a rolling stone.
Better late than to break.'

A flash from the lighthouse on the southern end of Ailsa
  Craig
when, all of a sudden, one of the ruffians
stood a little apart from the ruffian-ruck
and, stately at the vibraphone,

began to play what sounded like 'The Wild Colonial
  Boy'
while another held out his cap for a few spondulicks.
The sky was clearing now over Troy
as the Hennessys continued their talkee-talkee

about my waist-line
and their plans for *le weekend*.
The waiter's under-his-breath '*macaron*

nesoi' as my da searched for that announcement for the
  Orient Line
and from blessed Ailsa Craig, again from the southern
  end,
the foofooraw of two alternating foghorns.

'The beauty of it is that while the foofoorious pole-work
  of Charon
made the Wooroonooran cloudier
than the Styx or Acheron
and your da scoured the claims of a pig-gelder

and the schedule for the Portpatrick
passage and the price of cattle, polled and stripped,
and the proof against darnel and drawk
and this street arab

sang of the boy born and bred in Castlemaine,
Creusa, on whom you still had this adolescent crush,
passed some remark to a Hennessy about *"la senteur*

des faucilles" and, rather than "remain
in this unrealized plenitude", made a red rush
for the door, pausing only to air-kiss Hermia and
  Lysander.'

As she twinkled there for a moment, distant-near as
    Alpha Centauri,
I recognized the opening bars
not of 'Jane Shore' or 'Clerk Saunders'
but 'Waltzing Mathilda', played by some veteran of the
    Great War

on a mouth organ
and the waiter again drew himself up,
his threefold cord broken
at last, and my da took out a plug of Erinmore and a box
    of Bo-Peeps.

'For *"demain"*,' Virgil began to sing
with a rowley-powley gammon,
'read *"de Main"*. For "firse" read "frise".

For "Diamantina" read "Darling".
For "campana" read "campagna".
For "phosphorescence" read "phosphorus".'

Having looked in vain for the timetables of those P&O
   ferries
my da folded *The Tyrone Courier*, turned up the collar
   of the Abercrombie and Fitch
greatcoat that set him apart from the generality of
   frieze,
tossed back his glib the better to strike a match,

set the match to his pipeful of Erinmore
and thrust his hands into his pockets.
'For "lemur" read "femur".
For "braked" read "baked".' The cow-pony's innards
   packed

themselves back into the manganese-
red suitcase that would never now burst open on the
   border
of Queensland and wherever. 'For "samo"

read "soma'. For *"macaron nesoi"* read *"makaron*
   nesoi".'
Creusa bundling herself up in the shortest of short
   order,
and then some.

'For "maxims",' Virgil again drew himself up, 'read
    "Maxime's".
For "flint" read "skint".
The beauty of it is that your da and that other phantasm
no more set foot in Queensland

than the cat that got the cream
might look at a king. That's the sheer beauty of it.
Ne'er cast a clout, heigh, in mid-stream.
No brilliant. No brilliantine, ho. No classifieds

in *The Tyrone Courier*.
No billabong. No billy-boil.
No stately at the autoharp.

No Mastercard. No mainferre. No slopes of
    Montparnasse. No spare
the rod and spoil
the horse lost for want, heigh ho, of enough rope.'

A scattering to the four winds of the street arabs.
Creusa cutting me an intolerable deal
of slack as she gave me a wave of her razor-sharp
middle claw, half appalled, half in appeal,

and slipped forever from my arms.
'For "errata",' Virgil smiled, 'read "corrigenda".'
He looked straight through me to Lysander and Hermia.
'For "Mathilda" read "Matilda".

For "lass" read "less".
Time nor tide wait for a wink
from the aura

of Ailsa Craig. For "Menalaus" read "Menelaus".
For "dinkum" read "dink".
For "Wooroonooran", my darlings, read "Wirra Wirra".'